C000245867

*Greater Than a To
available in Ebook a

Greater Than a Tourist Book Series
Reviews from Readers

I think the series is wonderful and beneficial for tourists to get information before visiting the city.

-Seckin Zumbul, Izmir Turkey

I am a world traveler who has read many trip guides but this one really made a difference for me. I would call it a heartfelt creation of a local guide expert instead of just a guide.

-Susy, Isla Holbox, Mexico

New to the area like me, this is a must have!

-Joe, Bloomington, USA

This is a good series that gets down to it when looking for things to do at your destination without having to read a novel for just a few ideas.

-Rachel, Monterey, USA

Good information to have to plan my trip to this destination.

-Pennie Farrell, Mexico

Great ideas for a port day.

-Mary Martin USA

Aptly titled, you won't just be a tourist after reading this book. You'll be greater than a tourist!

-Alan Warner, Grand Rapids, USA

Even though I only have three days to spend in San Miguel in an upcoming visit, I will use the author's suggestions to guide some of my time there. An easy read - with chapters named to guide me in directions I want to go.

-Robert Catapano, USA

Great insights from a local perspective! Useful information and a very good value!

-Sarah, USA

This series provides an in-depth experience through the eyes of a local. Reading these series will help you to travel the city in with confidence and it'll make your journey a unique one.

-Andrew Teoh, Ipoh, Malaysia

GREATER THAN A TOURIST- SYDNEY NEW SOUTH WALES AUSTRALIA

50 Travel Tips from a Local

Laura-Jo Thorpe

CZYK Publishing Since 2011.

Greater Than a Tourist

Lock Haven, PA
All rights reserved.

ISBN: 9781712470862

>TOURIST

50 TRAVEL TIPS FROM A LOCAL

BOOK DESCRIPTION

Are you excited about planning your next trip? Do you want to try something new? Would you like some guidance from a local? If you answered yes to any of these questions, then this Greater Than a Tourist book is for you. *Greater Than a Tourist-New South Wales Australia* by Author Laura-Jo Thorpe offers the inside scoop on Sydney. Most travel books tell you how to travel like a tourist. Although there is nothing wrong with that, as part of the Greater Than a Tourist series, this book will give you travel tips from someone who has lived at your next travel destination.

In these pages, you will discover advice that will help you throughout your stay. This book will not tell you exact addresses or store hours but instead will give you excitement and knowledge from a local that you may not find in other smaller print travel books.

Travel like a local. Slow down, stay in one place, and get to know the people and culture. By the time you finish this book, you will be eager and prepared to travel to your next destination.

Inside this travel guide book you will find:

- Insider tips from a local.

- Packing and planning list.

- List of travel questions to ask yourself or others while traveling.

- A place to write your travel bucket list.

OUR STORY

Traveling is a passion of the Greater than a Tourist book series creator. Lisa studied abroad in college, and for their honeymoon Lisa and her husband toured Europe. During her travels to Malta, an older man tried to give her some advice based on his own experience living on the island since he was a young boy. She was not sure if she should talk to the stranger but was interested in his advice. When traveling to some places she was wary to talk to locals because she was afraid that they weren't being genuine. Through her travels, Lisa learned how much locals had to share with tourists. Lisa created the Greater Than a Tourist book series to help connect people with locals. A topic that locals are very passionate about sharing.

TABLE OF CONTENTS

11. BECOME A SUNDAY (OR ANY DAY), DRIVER
12. WHEN IN DOUBT, PEDAL IT OUT
13. WHEREVER YOU LAY YOUR HAT…
14. BE A HAPPY CAMPER
15. PAY YOUR RESPECTS TO THE ELDERS
16. GO ON AN ABORIGINAL CULTURE WALKS
17. COME ON IN, THE WATER IS FINE
18. GO TO CIRCULAR QUAY
19. WATCH A SHOW AT THE OPERA HOUSE
20. HANG AROUND AT THE GIANT 'COATHANGER'
21. TAKE THE FERRY TO MANLY
22. SNORKEL AT SHELLEY BEACH
23. MAKE THE CROSSING TO THE COVE
24. STOP OFF AT THE OAKS
25. STOP OFF AT THE OAKS
26. GET SOME FISH AND CHIPS
27. GO WEST
28. BE WET 'N' WILD FOR A DAY
29. AT THE HEART OF THE MATTER
30. SHHHH…IT'S A SECRET
31. REACH FOR THE STARS
32. STROLL THROUGH THE ROYAL BOTANIC GARDEN
33. CYCLE AROUND CENTENNIAL PARK

DEDICATION

This book is dedicated to Jim, my travel buddy, and global partner in crime.

ABOUT THE AUTHOR

Laura-Jo is a Brit abroad who decided to ditch the UK drizzle in search of sunnier climes and adventure. Since leaving London in 2015, she has enjoyed lots of travelling and, after finishing a 2-year stint in South East Asia, has set her sights on seeing the rest of the world, one continent at a time (whilst conquering her fear of flying!).

Whilst working as a primary school teacher, she is currently living with the rest of the Brit-pack in Bondi Beach, Sydney. Laura-Jo loves reading, cooking, and finding new sea pools along the coast where she can relax and enjoy the Australian sunshine.

Her ideal holiday is packed with wildlife spotting, cocktail drinking, and plenty of swimming.

HOW TO USE THIS BOOK

The *Greater Than a Tourist* book series was written by someone who has lived in an area for over three months. The goal of this book is to help travelers either dream or experience different locations by providing opinions from a local. The author has made suggestions based on their own experiences. Please check before traveling to the area in case the suggested places are unavailable.

Travel Advisories: As a first step in planning any trip abroad, check the Travel Advisories for your intended destination.
https://travel.state.gov/content/travel/en/traveladvisories/traveladvisories.html

FROM THE PUBLISHER

Traveling can be one of the most important parts of a person's life. The anticipation and memories that you have are some of the best. As a publisher of the Greater Than a Tourist, as well as the popular *50 Things to Know* book series, we strive to help you learn about new places, spark your imagination, and inspire you. Wherever you are and whatever you do I wish you safe, fun, and inspiring travel.

Lisa Rusczyk Ed. D.
CZYK Publishing

WELCOME TO
> TOURIST

INTRODUCTION

"Australia is just so full of surprises."

— Bill Bryson

Sydney
New South Wales, Australia

S o, you've decided to book a holiday to Sydney, Australia but now you're not sure where to start because, frankly, there are just too many things to see and do. It can be overwhelming to plan a trip and it's hard to choose what to do and what to miss out. However, help is at hand! Here are some top tips on things you should know and what you should experience while you're visiting one of my favourite cities in the world.

Sydney Climate

	High	Low
January	79	66
February	79	67
March	77	64
April	73	59
May	68	53
June	63	49
July	63	47
August	65	48
September	69	53
October	72	57
November	74	60
December	78	64

GreaterThanaTourist.com

Temperatures are in Fahrenheit degrees.
Source: NOAA

1. IN THE WORDS OF BAZ LUHRMANN, "WEAR SUNSCREEN"

Let's start with the basics, kids. Sun safety is a total must out here in 'Straya. You'll see so much naked skin over here; it'll blow your minds. But anyone who is smart will have covered all that delightful dermis in some factor 50. At this point, some of you are shaking your head and thinking, "I don't burn, I'll just buy factor 20". Or maybe you're one of those extra confident sun worshippers considering getting some tanning oil and working on a killer tan, well remember this, you have been warned! The sun down-under is crazy strong. Even when it's cloudy, it's still working its way towards giving you some serious sunburn so be cool, stay smothered in sun cream, and aim for the higher numbers,—you won't regret it.

2. STAY CONNECTED WITH A LOCAL SIM CARD

There are a wide variety of tourist sim cards available from the moment you clear customs. If you want a bit more variety when it comes to providers; wait until you've left the airport and pick one up from a 7Eleven, Woolworths, Coles, and most local newsagents. Obviously, you need to be sure that your phone is unlocked before you can make the most of these offers. Using a local SIM card will ensure you don't get ripped off on roaming fees when you finish your holiday and step back into reality back home. It also means that you can find your way around Sydney easily using maps and any of the shared transport apps (more about that later).

3. DRUNK IN LOVE (BUT NOT ON THE BEACH)

Sydney has some beautiful coastal beaches and you'd be forgiven for thinking that they are the best places to chill out at the end of the day with a cold beer, especially while you watch the sun go down.

But, if you do that, you'll be at risk from some unwanted attention from the police. That's right folks; most public spaces (including parks and beaches) are alcohol-free zones. If you are caught with booze, you risk having it taken away and could get fined $220. These rules also apply for public events. There is usually security at the gates of these types of occasions and they will do bag searches. So, don't waste your time or your money, leave the bottles at home!

4. GET A LITTLE SAND BETWEEN YOUR TOES

Home to some of the most iconic shorelines in the world, Sydney has a plethora of beaches to choose from (more on these later). So, you should consider spending a huge proportion of your holiday relaxing by the sea. However, as with a lot of things in Sydney, the beach can be delightful, but dangerous if you're careless. I don't want to put a dampener on your sun time/fun time, but I sadly read a lot of articles in the local paper about people who have had accidents at the beach because they didn't understand some important facts about the sea.

There are always signs about specific marine life that you should be aware of in the area of your choosing. Jellyfish are pretty common and come in a variety of shapes and sizes, but there will be warnings up if there are lots of jellies floating around. The same goes for sharks. The lifeguards are super vigilant about the dreaded dorsal fin, so you can enjoy your swim without fear of Jaws joining you. However, if there is a shark around, you'll hear a warning siren and it is, of course, best to vacate the water intermediately. Also, your local news network will be quick on the draw when it comes to reporting shark sightings, so that everyone is in the loop.

Most importantly, the real thing to be wise of while you're enjoying the waves is the rip tides. They are strong, ruthless, and annoyingly difficult to spot. Look out for a rippled surface within calm smooth waters and dark-coloured water. They have a strong pull and if you are caught in one, the most important thing to do is remain calm. Raise one arm to alert the lifeguards. If possible, try to swim parallel to the shore to get out of the rip. Don't stress though, the lifeguards are trained to spot distress and their response times are super-fast.

5. OUT IN THE BUSH

You haven't experienced Australia until you've strapped on your walking boots and hit the bush trails. Sydney has numerous bush walks to choose from. From short ones for beginners to long winding trails that take hours to complete. Take some time to research national parks and local walks to find a suitable track that works for you and your fitness level. If you are hitting the dirt, remember to keep your phone charged, understand and plan your journey well ahead of time, and keep hydrated. It is also important to keep on the established tracks and not wander off—however tempting it might be to take a little shortcut!

6. EVERYTHING IN AUSTRALIA WANTS TO KILL YOU

.....But there aren't too many things in the city that are hugely dangerous, to be totally honest. Do not let this particular tip put you off. The Land Down Under is a fantastic place with tons of gorgeous places to go and to see. However, there are still some creepy crawlies and slithery suckers that you should be aware of before arriving. There are some beautiful parks and bush walks around, but be sure to keep your eyes peeled for the Eastern Brown Snake; the delightfully named Common Death Adder; and the Funnel Web Spider. If you're off to the beach, there is always the risk of being swimming buddies with the blue-ringed octopus; box jellyfish; and/or bull sharks. While there are many perils here, there is also plenty of information around telling you how to deal with and identify each hostile creature. Don't be afraid. Be adventurous, but be aware!

Now, that the doom and gloom and warnings are out of the way, let us get on with the fun stuff.

7. GO WILD FOR THE WILDLIFE

Australia has some seriously weird, and chronically adorable, critters. So, we need to do a quick rundown of the who's who and what's what in the animal kingdom. Nature's teddy bear—and possibly the cutest thing out there—is Koalas; who can be spotted high up in the trees, chilling out, maxing, and relaxing on some eucalyptus. However, sometimes, they can be seen on the road, and these are the times you need to know what to do. Make sure to pull over and be safe. At this point, do an internet search for the nearest koala carer or call out company. They will probably give you some info on what to do next but in case they don't; approach the animal carefully and cover it with a blanket or basket. Remember; koalas have sharp claws and will be scared. Just stay with it until the service you have called arrives. Whatever you do—and however tempting it is—do not try to stroke it!

8. TIE ME KANGAROO DOWN, SPORT

If you end up heading out onto the open road and getting out of the city, then chances are, you will see something furry hopping across the horizon. Congratulations! You've spotted your first Kangaroo (or wallaby). Now that you've seen it, try not to run into one when you're driving at night because rental car damage can be really pricey when you give the car back. The best way to avoid accidents is by not driving around dusk or after sundown, but if you can't do this, then stay alert and drive slowly.

What else do you need to know about these marvellous macro-pods? Aussies eat Roo. There's no getting away from it. Check out your nearest Woolies for a selection of Kangaroo steaks, burgers, and kebabs. If you're an adventurous eater (and you aren't a vegetarian), then I'd say give it a go, you only live once right? If you're planning on throwing a Roo on the barbie; then I'll tell you a local secret, marinade it in cola first. It tastes divine!

Granted, I'm sure that some of you won't want to head out into the bush or see your first kangaroo served up to you on a plate, so you can always pop over to The Basin in Pittwater, Featherdale Wildlife Park or Taronga Zoo.

9. LEARN THE LINGO

Aussies love an abbreviation. I've had so much fun learning the words and terms they use for different things. If you're devastated, you're devo. Heading to the beach? Pack your cozzie (or your swimmers, depending on where you're from). Are you a vegetarian who loves avocado in the afternoon? Then you're a vego who loves avo in the arvo. The locals are so laid back here; it's too much effort to say the whole word. Pretty soon, you'll be speaking like a local too, it's just too much trouble not to try.

10. TAP ON, TAP OFF

If you want to get around the city on the bus, train, ferry, and/or light rail, you're going to need an Opal card. Pick one up from a newsagent or a station. Remember that there is a 5 AUD charge for the card itself and a lot of retailers require you to pay a minimum. Mostly, you'll need either a Black Opal card for Adults or a Green one for children (age 4-15). Now that you've purchased your card, you're good to go. Getting the bus is made much simpler with an Opal because there are very few services that take cash on board, preferring to be 'Prepay Only'. Just remember you need to tap off the bus when you leave, otherwise, you will be charged for a full journey.

11. BECOME A SUNDAY (OR ANY DAY), DRIVER

If you want to get around at your own pace or you just love driving, you can use one of the shared car schemes to fulfil all your motor needs. Shared cars are a great way to get around the city or if you're thinking of getting out into the outback. Schemes such as Carnextdoor are free to sign up for; there is no ongoing membership fee and with loads of different types of vehicles dotted around the city, it is incredibly convenient and easy to use. You simply need to be over 21, have a clean license, and have been driving for over 2 years.

It couldn't be easier to use these cars, you search for the type of car you need, find one nearby and Carnextdoor will send you an unlock code 15 minutes before the time you've requested the car. Be sure to download the app to ensure maximum easiness. Each car has a lock box (usually hanging off one of the windows) that is, for some reason, named Fred. You type in your code, Fred opens up and, boom, you have the keys to your new ride.

Most of the cars also have e-Tags in them, which means you can drive on the toll roads and the tag will record the cost which you'll pay for at the end of your rental period. You can update the time on the app if you think you're going to be late so that you don't get charged, just make sure you fill up the fuel tank before you end your journey.

12. WHEN IN DOUBT, PEDAL IT OUT

If you're a touch health conscious or eco-friendly, then perhaps bike-sharing is more your thing. Sydney has a great variety of shared bike systems. You'll see the bikes dotted around all over the city. Its super simple to use these cycles and there are currently at least 4 apps to choose from. As there are pros and cons to each company; it is best to Google each one yourself when you arrive and decide which one best suits you. Some important rules to remember once you've made your choice are; always wear a helmet, do not cycle in the bus-only lanes, and lastly, if you're riding at night, make sure the bike has working lights at the back and front. Lastly, get on your bike, have an awesome time and feel the wind in your hair!

13. WHEREVER YOU LAY YOUR HAT...

Just like other well-visited travel destinations, there are a wide variety of places to crash in the city. Of course, there are hundreds of hotels to choose from as well as hostels if you are on a bit of a tighter budget.

However, if you really want to feel like a local, then you should live like a local! Sydney has a thriving AirBnB scene and there are some great choices available; from modern, spacious apartments in and around the Central Business District, to luxury yachts, enchanted caves, and your very own private tree house. As a BnBer myself, I think it's my duty to mention at this point that, if you choose to go down the short-term private rental route; please ensure you are respectful while staying in the property and don't have obnoxiously loud parties or break things.

14. BE A HAPPY CAMPER

Outdoor lovers, rejoice! Sydney has an abundance of captivating camping spots for you to roll out your sleeping bag and toast your marshmallows. Whether you like to Glamp it up or sleep under the stars, there is something for everyone at the National Parks, beaches, and even zoos in the Harbour City.

Only 15 minutes from the Opera House and steeped in history, Cockatoo Island is a unique spot that can only be reached by ferry. You can either pitch your own tent or go glam in their luxury tents. Similarly, there are many camping spots at parks and beaches such as Bents Basin, Putty Beach, and Lake Cove. And for the animal lovers, there is always the (rather pricey) Roar and Snore at Taronga Zoo.

15. PAY YOUR RESPECTS TO THE ELDERS

Sydney has a fascinating and rich history, and you should get yourself educated by planning a trip to some of the many different Aboriginal museums and art galleries. If you find yourself at Bondi beach, you can pop into the Coo-ee Aboriginal Art Gallery on Lamrock Avenue, which shows artefacts and historical bark painting—as well as contemporary artwork. A little further out West, you can find the Kate Owen Gallery or the Muru Mittigar Aboriginal Cultural Centre, where you can find out about the local tribes and do nature walks. It is definitely worth the train fare.

16. GO ON AN ABORIGINAL CULTURE WALKS

While galleries and museums are a great way to learn about the past, some people prefer to get out and about to experience history while on the move. For those people, there are lots of other ways to experience Aboriginal culture. If you're a walker, check out The Rocks Dreaming Aboriginal Heritage Tour. If sailing is more your thing, then try the Aboriginal Cultural Cruise Clark Island. While we're on the subject of walking, download the Sydney Culture Walks app; it's another great way to see the cities secrets and history.

17. COME ON IN, THE WATER IS FINE

Although there are some of the most beautiful beaches in the world here, I, for one, absolutely hate sand. It gets everywhere and you are vacuuming it up for days on end. But Sydney has floods of sea pools so if you're like me, you can still enjoy the splash without the sand. Here is a short rundown of some of the most bewitching baths around the bay.

Mahon Pool is a beautiful pool down in Maroubra that is always popular with the locals. Hidden from view, it is the ideal spot for a picnic and has gorgeous views. For those who favour more subdued spots, then Malabar Pool might be the place for you. Clovelly Beach is perfect for snorkelers and marine life lovers, while North Sydney Olympic pool has epic views of the Harbour Bridge, and its ladies only at McIvers Baths at Coogee Beach.

18. GO TO CIRCULAR QUAY

I won't spend too much time on this because Circular Quay is hardly a secret but I could hardly leave it out now could I? Full of street performers and tourists snapping pictures, the Quay is a hive of activity. Looming over the harbour will probably be one of the impressively large cruise ships that dock regularly pouring out tourists and taking up space. You can also find the Museum of Contemporary Art which always has an exciting choice of free or paid-for exhibits to get your artistic juices flowing.

Being the birthplace of modern Sydney, The Rocks is steeped in history and has the fascinating Discovery museum on Kendall Lane; which tells the story of the early settlers. Once you've had your fill of the past, you can peruse for presents and trinkets at the market, usually held at the weekend—although they have a food market on Fridays.

19. WATCH A SHOW AT THE OPERA HOUSE

Built-in 1959 and completing every tourists Australian holiday photo album ever since the Sydney Opera House is an absolute must on your list of things to do and see. Housed inside those famous white sails are different spaces and stages where you can see concerts, dance, theatre and, of course, opera. You can also do either a 1-hour guided tour or a 2-hour 'backstage' tour. There are loads of bars and restaurants around that area, but you should be warned that they are pretty pricey, although you should do it at least once. Also, it gets absolutely rammed on Friday evenings with all the office workers wanting to chill out after a hard week of slog, so make sure to get there early so you can get a seat.

A great little tip for money-saving tourists is to check out sites such as Groupon as they sometimes have cheap deals for specific shows.

20. HANG AROUND AT THE GIANT 'COATHANGER'

Speaking of iconic sites, make sure you head to the Harbour Bridge for some super snaps. Standing at 134 metres high, you absolutely can't miss this quintessential image of Sydney, which really holds its own in the skyline. If you're a thrill seeker (and happy to spend a fair amount), then you can hook yourself up to the BridgeClimb and trek up to the top. Don't bother to take your cameras with you though, because they are strictly not allowed. They have official photographers who will snap you a pic when you reach the summit.

Perhaps you don't really fancy the price tag and prefer to keep your bucks in your back pocket? If that's the case, then the Pylon Lookout is the place for you. It costs considerably less than the BridgeClimb and has equally beautiful views once you've ascended the 200 steps to the top. You'll also find information about how the bridge was built; which is a useful distraction for when you're trying to catch your breath after that climb!

For the young at heart, stop off at Luna Park for some fairground fun as well. Its cliché, but its enjoyable and the children will love it.

21. TAKE THE FERRY TO MANLY

Don't forget to whip out your Opal card, hop on the ferry, and spend a day at Manly. It is easy to lose time in this glorious little slice of heaven. Whet your whistle on the 4 Pines Brewery Tour, which starts at 12:30 pm sharp, before grabbing lunch at Hemmingway's, a charming book-inspired cafe and restaurant with charming views and excellent craft beers. Afterwards, walk off your lunch at the Manly Dam for those in need of some outdoor pursuit, brush up on your culture at the Manly Art Gallery and Museum or take the plunge at the Sea Life Sanctuary.

22. SNORKEL AT SHELLEY BEACH

If you made the trip over to Manly, then be sure to pack your diving mask and snorkel. Just a short walk away from the main beach in Manly, and forming part of Cabbage Tree Bay Aquatic Reserve, Shelley beach is a charming little corner of the world. Snorkelers and scuba divers alike can enjoy the stunning sea life and families will appreciate the calm waters.

Once you've spent the day collecting shells and exploring the headland, it's time to treat yourself to some sundowners at the Boathouse, a gorgeous little restaurant and bar that serves tasty cocktails and is full of beachside charm.

23. MAKE THE CROSSING TO THE COVE

Sydney-siders are guilty of rarely making the trip over the bridge to the northern suburbs, so don't make the same mistake. There are some beautiful parks and beaches to be seen, including Lane Cove. You'll find a variety of camping sites here and lots to do. There is a multitude of pleasing picnic spots and you can walk off your lunch by choosing to explore one of the exciting bushwalks. Perhaps you prefer site-seeing on the move? Then there are a couple of cycle paths that snake around the park or you could float down the river on your own kayak.

24. STOP OFF AT THE OAKS

Before you make your way back over the Harbour Bridge and leave the northern parts of Sydney behind you, be sure to stop off for a drink in The Oaks Hotel. Best enjoyed in the evening, grab a craft beer from one of the bars and get a seat in the garden. There you will find a magical atmosphere once the sun has gone down and the giant old oak tree is lit up with thousands of fairy lights. They also have a great food menu there or you can request to use one of the barbeques.

25. STOP OFF AT THE OAKS

Before you make your way back over the Harbour Bridge and leave the northern parts of Sydney behind you, be sure to stop off for a drink in The Oaks Hotel. Best enjoyed in the evening, grab a craft beer from one of the bars and get a seat in the garden. There you will find a magical atmosphere once the sun has gone down and the giant old oak tree is lit up with thousands of fairy lights. They also have a great food menu there or you can request to use one of the barbeques.

26. GET SOME FISH AND CHIPS

Although I love to travel far and wide to sample local weird and wonderful cuisines, sometimes I get a pang of homesickness. Luckily for me, and hundreds of other comfort eaters, Australians know how to do good fish and chips. Of course, there are lots of places to deal with this particular craving but, in my humble opinion; the best place in Sydney is The Bottom of the Harbour, which has been frying fish for over 20 years. The permanent queue for golden, fried goodness is a sure sign of its popularity with the locals. Pick up a take away, cross over the road, and enjoy your dinner while sitting on Balmoral Beach and looking out onto North Head.

27. GO WEST

Sydney is a big place and you could be forgiven for thinking that all the action is in the centre, but there's fun to be had in the West too, you just have to know where to go.

If you love all things retro then unpack that poodle skirt and grease back your quiff for a night out at the Skyline Drive-in Cinema, Blacktown. The prices vary depending on how many people per car but sitting under the stars, cuddling up to your date, and ordering a malt shake at the Happy Days-inspired restaurant will make it totally worth the cost.

Those of you who are young at heart can also try bouncing into action at the Jump Zone Revolution, which is in Gregory Hills and offers 4 different exciting jump zones to choose from. Western Sydney also offers the Riverside Theatres, Parramatta Park and Museum of Fire, meaning there is a little something for everyone to enjoy.

28. BE WET 'N' WILD FOR A DAY

If you like nothing better than floating about on a lazy river or tubing down some extreme slides, then make sure to pencil in some time at Sydney's Wet 'n' Wild Waterpark. Here, you will find lots of different rides and pools to suit all tastes. Whether you're a group of fun lovers or a solo rider, young and old alike will enjoy a day frolicking in their swimwear.

You will need $12 for a locker and they have free sunscreen stations all around the park so it makes it easy to be sun safe. You can take in picnic food, so pack an esky, but no hot food or alcohol is allowed. Take a big bottle of water with you as well to stay hydrated. Beat the long and boring queues by using your wristband to book in a time for the ride of your choice, that way, you can go off and enjoy the rest of the park and use the express line when your chosen time comes around. Of course, you can pay to use the express queues all the time, without waiting but using the booking system for a time slot is free so make use of that and save your money for something else!

29. AT THE HEART OF THE MATTER

The CBD in Sydney is full of the usual hustle and bustle, and also provides some great spots for shopping. It has some great sites to see, including the Town Hall in Spring, when the building is surrounded by vivid purple Jacaranda trees in full bloom.

You can also walk the Good Lines, which were once used as a freight rail system but are now home to a beautiful public space. Here you will find a great selection of interesting architecture as you play table tennis or with your little ones in the children's water play area. It is also really close to the Powerhouse Museum, so regularly has pop up events.

30. SHHHH...IT'S A SECRET

Everybody loves a treasure hunt and the great thing about this one is that there is a drink at the end of it. Sydney has lots of hidden bars, all very different and all great. Mojo Record Bar not only provides great drinks (and free sweets to nibble on while you're getting a round in) but you can also pick up some great vinyls and LPs in the shop at the front, so be sure to keep your eyes peeled for this little banger. Similarly hidden in plain sight is Grandma's Bar, a tropical, tiki-inspired paradise beneath the streets. It's easy to miss so keep your eyes low and look for the entrance near The Guitar Lounge. Other great places to try are The Baxter Inn (for all you whiskey lovers out there) and Uncle Ming's for its trendy, oriental inspired décor.

31. REACH FOR THE STARS

One of my favourite places in the city, Observatory Hill is the perfect place to sit and enjoy some people watching, whilst taking in the stunning scenery. Make sure you're around for when the sun is going down as that will score you some excellent photos for the holiday album. At the top of the hill, the city's Observatory looks out over the rooftops and is a really interesting place to walk around. I would highly recommend booking a night tour as you will get a chance to use some of the different telescopes for a real eye-opening view of the cosmos.

32. STROLL THROUGH THE ROYAL BOTANIC GARDEN

There are a number of gorgeous green parks and gardens around Sydney, but topping the charts for me is the Royal Botanic Garden. They have free walks that provide some really interesting facts and information about the different trees and plants in the park. The walks usually start at 10:30 am from the Garden Shop. Make sure to spend some time in the Succulent Garden and listen out for the fascinating story about the Wollemi Pines.

33. CYCLE AROUND CENTENNIAL PARK

Assuming that you're not bored of parks at this point, exploring Centennial Park is a great way to spend the day. Spanning over 360 hectares, there is something for everyone here. Surrounding the whole park is a dedicated bike and rollerblade lane, making it easy for fitness fanatics and fun seekers to go at their own pace without being bullied out of the way by those pesky car drivers. Tourists with families can while away the hours at the Ian Potter Children's

Playground which is a great little self-contained children's space that has sand pits, water features to play in, and a whole host of interesting climbing frames to keep your children entertained. Other great features of this magnificent park include, but are not limited to; horse and pony rides, a whole host of kids activities and the Entertainment Quarter, where you can grab a bite to eat and see a movie in the cinema.

34. CATCH A GAME

Aussies love a bit of sport and there are lots of opportunities to go and watch a live game when you visit. Even if you're not a sports fan (of which, I can include myself in that category) the atmosphere and the energy are not to be missed out on. You can choose from the Waverley Oval, the Allianz Stadium or the huge Olympic Stadium to choose from. Now, all you've got to do is work out whether you're an NRL, AFL, NBL or A-League kind of person!

35. GET A ROUND IN AT A PUB QUIZ

Get that grey matter working by testing your knowledge at a local pub quiz. There are options all over the city on any day of the week. Specifically, my favourite pub quiz is the Lord Dudley Pub on Thursday nights in Woolhara. This cosy little English-style pub serves tasty food and the bartenders pull good pints. Thursday is usually $10 burger night and the Quiz host, Jarred, is a hoot. The action kicks off at 7pm so make sure to get yourself settled on a good table before that and enjoy!

36. PERFECT YOUR BARBEQUING SKILLS

Sydney is littered with public barbeques and with good reason. The weather is pretty much always perfect for throwing some shrimps on the barbie and cooking up a storm. Never say that to an Aussie though because it's a huge cliché and besides, they aren't shrimps, they're prawns. Anyway, back to the BBQs. Some of the best beach grills are at Shelley

Beach and The Basin, while you can find ideally placed hot plates at dotted around pretty much every park in the city and surrounds. Grills are usually cleaned every morning, but it's considered courteous to clean up after yourself, wiping the plates down and scraping excess debris off. General rules of thumb as ever when you are eating outdoors is to dispose of your rubbish and leave it as you would like to find it; clean and inviting.

37. SIGN UP

If you want to keep up-to-date on activities and events happening when you are visiting the city, then it is a good idea to sign up to mailing lists such as The Urban List or Concrete Playground. These types of website are dedicated to keeping its subscribers in the know about the latest pop up event or the most desirable bars and restaurants to visit. They give terrific tips on what's on and what's not to be missed—as well as giving advice on what to avoid. You'll be hard pressed to find a local who isn't signed up to one of these or similar sites, it's the ideal way to keep in the know.

38. SEE SOME FLICKS AT THE RITZ

Possibly one of the cheapest—and definitely one of the most interesting cinema spaces in Sydney—the Ritz Cinema in Randwick is a fantastic way to spend an evening. Here is my usual itinerary for an evening in Randwick; arrive with plenty of time before the film to get a drink at The Bat Country, a Hunter S. Thompson-themed bar opposite the cinema. Or have some cocktails in the Ritz Bar, which can be found above the cinema and serves excellent movie-inspired cocktails. Once you've drained your drink, grab your tickets, and settle in to watch your film. Once the film is over, progress to one of the many restaurants that surround the cinema to chow down on some dinner while discussing the film's pros and cons, just to finish off a lovely evening.

39. BYO

Most people enjoy a tipple with their meal of an evening, but sometimes it's nice to have your absolute favourite brand of vino. Well, there are lots of places that offer 'bring your own bottle' policies, so you can enjoy your meal knowing you don't have to pay over the odds for a usually cheap bottle of plonk. Scattered all over the city, BYO restaurants are a blessing for the budget-conscious. If you're in Bondi, the best place for BYO is Bangkok Bites; a Thai infusion place that is always busy and has some mouth-watering options. Other fab options are The Sultans Table, Enmore (for Turkish cuisine) and Rosso Pomodoro Italian, Balmain; both of which offer no corkage charge!

40. PLAN YOUR ESCAPE

On the rare occasion that the weather isn't optimal for sunbathing or surfing, tourists and locals alike need a way to get through the day. Sydney has a great range of escape rooms to keep you entertained—at least for a short amount of time. I've broken down some of the best the city has to offer according to skill level:

Mission Sydney – Book the Vampire castle if you're a newbie (or if you don't want something too taxing).

Next Level – This one is for literary lovers. Book the 15-minute Blitz Room for a warm up before moving onto one of the other rooms, for a lengthier stay.

Paniq Room – For professional puzzlers. Try your hand at Abandoned Military Bunker on the Rocks or Supercell 117.

41. GO WHALE WATCHING

Sydney is well-known for its whale season. Usually, between May and December, these underwater giants migrate along the coast and it sure is a sight to behold.

You'll see so many different whale watching companies when you wonder around Circular Quay. Most offer a 2nd trip guarantee if you have been unlucky enough not to have spotted one on your first attempt. I can highly recommend a trip like this at least once while you are here. I personally saw some incredible breeches and had a lovely day. Although, a tip for the seasick prone, don't use the loos when its choppy, they are normally well-below deck and the motion is made a thousand times worse.

However, once you've done one paid for trip, that doesn't mean the end of your spotting adventures. There are several different places dotted along the shoreline where you might be lucky enough to see a few tell-tale friendly dorsal fins poking out. Try Hornby Lighthouse; which has a light (excuse the pun) and easy walking trail, or Cape Solander; which is where they complete the official whale counts, or The Royal National park, where you'll see a ton of exciting wildlife as well!

42. BECOME A POD MEMBER

Technically this tip is not for Sydney, but it has to go on the bucket list of things to do in Australia. If spotting a whale from afar isn't good enough for you, then why not drive up to Port Stephens and get yourself a ticket for the Swim with Wild Dolphins tour. With this trip you'll be able to get into the sea and swim with a wild pod of dolphins. The company is heavily monitored to make sure they do not disrupt or harm the dolphins, so you can enjoy yourself safe in the knowledge that it is not affecting these beautiful creatures.

43. TREK ON A COASTAL WALKS

If you're a hiker, you'll be spoilt for choice when it comes to coastal walks in Sydney. There are so many to choose from, all with different pros (and cons) but if you want my advice, the two walks which are not to be missed are the following:

One of the most charming walks is the Rose Bay to Watsons Bay track. Start off at Rose Bay, stroll along and get some great views of the harbour, stop for a breather and maybe a dip in the sea pool at Nielsen Park, before finishing off at Watsons Bay; where you can get a ferry back to the city quite easily.

Popular with locals and tourists alike, don't miss out on the breath-taking views and excellent choice of sea pools that the classic Coogee to Bondi trail has to offer. When you're finished, you can reward yourself with a cold beer and some fish and chips at Icebergs, a Bondi institution.

44. SNAP YOURSELF HAPPY

We live in a digital age where, for some travellers, one of the most important things about a holiday is the quality of the photo album at the end. If you're a social media butterfly, then spend some time in Newton, where there is some incredible street art on pretty much every spare wall and corner. Or similarly, there's always some interesting temporary pieces lining the Bondi beach walls.

For nature lovers, the Chinese Friendship Garden has some stunning scenery. If you're into pics of your plate, try Speedos, in North Bondi and, if it's urban art you're after, stop off at the Forgotten Songs installation, at Angel Place.

45. BE BOWLED OVER

Sydney siders love a spot of lawn bowls. No longer just the sport of OAPS, this once typically British sport is now played all over Sydney by trendy bare-foot hipsters, and with good reason. The clubs are usually surrounded by sensational scenery and tend to serve enough booze and food to keep you going for at least a few games.

If you're anything like me and you can't bowl for toffee, make the most of the free training at Marrickville Bowling Club. Clovelly and The PBC are among the best spots, and The Greens in North Sydney has the Harbour Bridge as its backdrop.

46. DO BRUNCH

Not all holidays involve traipsing around the famous landmarks and taking in the local history. Brunch lovers should make Sunday their day of rest and spend some time at The Grounds, Alexandria. Host to a wonderful selection of artisan bakeries, vegetable gardens and a small animal farm as well as coffee shops, restaurants, and market stalls, The Grounds is an ideal—and popular—Sunday pursuit. Get there early to avoid big queues and make sure to stop by and say hi to Kevin Bacon, the resident pig!

47. HANG TEN

It goes without saying that if you spend any time at the beach on your holiday, you should probably give surfing a shot. You'll be able to get lessons on most of the larger beaches. Trained instructors will show you the basics on the sand first, and when you're ready, you'll be able to take to the waves. It is hard work, but fun and rewarding, so definitely worth it.

48. SHOP TILL YOU DROP

Sydney has a marvellous market scene so be sure to spend some time scouring the stalls for bargains and sampling delicious dishes. You'll often hear people talking about Paddy's Market, allegedly one of Sydney's best but I don't rate it myself. It's too crowded and full of typical tacky souvenirs. For some more original gifts and mementos, stop off in Paddington every Saturday, or Bondi markets every weekend. Second hand seekers should give Rozelle a go; also open all weekend, or Surry Hills, which happens on the first Saturday of the month.

Food lovers, try something new at the first Sydney Vegan market, Marrickville, on the third Sunday of every month and night owls, swoop by the family friendly Eastwood Night Markets on Saturday evenings.

49. THE BLUE MOUNTAINS AND BEYOND

No Sydney break is complete without a tour of the famous Blue Mountains or the Hunter Valley. The best way to see these are to book trips which depart from various places around the city on a regular basis. The tours can be a little expensive but are worth it as the journeys to and from these locations are long and tedious and you'll want to partake in the free wine and beers samples safely. Do a bit of research into the itineraries of each tour as some provide lunch and others offer paid extras, so you can be sure you've booked the right one for your interests (and budgets). You can hike the trails of the renowned Three Sisters, steeped in Aboriginal history and perfect for fitness fans or relax in the day spas if strenuous exercise isn't your thing. I would recommend the Glow Worm cave tours, although they are short, it really is a fascinating and a beautiful spectacle.

50. WHEN TO COME

Booking the perfect holiday means being smart about when to travel. September to November is the start of spring so the weather is cooler but beautiful and accommodation won't be overly expensive. Once you move into December and January, you will be paying through the nose for even the smallest of places because with Christmas, the New Year firework display and Chinse New Year, these are some of the most popular months to holiday here. June to August is low season, so you'll find cheap deals on flights and tours as well as more choice for your accommodation.

Activity wise, Sydney Festival kicks off the year in January and has lots of different events across the city, including music and performances. Vivid festival happens from May and June and is the only winter festival Sydney has. It transforms the Opera house into a coloured canvas of bright lights and dazzling designs and will be a delightful addition to your holiday photo album.

Finally, music lovers, take your pick from Bluesfest, The Secret Garden Party, Subsonic, Days Like This and Harbour Life are only a few of the most popular music festivals on offer, you'll be spoilt for choice!

TOP REASONS TO BOOK THIS TRIP

Beaches: Surf, chill, sunbathe, paddle. Sydney beaches are world famous for a reason, you know.

Breakfast. Smashed avocado on toast with fresh coffee. Best. Breakfast. You'll. Ever. Have!

Booze. Brimming with wine tours, breweries and bottle shops, your Sydney trip promises to be a tipsy one.

PACKING AND PLANNING TIPS

A Week before Leaving

- Arrange for someone to take care of pets and water plants.

- Email and Print important Documents.

- Get Visa and vaccines if needed.

- Check for travel warnings.

- Stop mail and newspaper.

- Notify Credit Card companies where you are going.

- Passports and photo identification is up to date.

- Pay bills.

- Copy important items and download travel Apps.

- Start collecting small bills for tips.

- Have post office hold mail while you are away.

- Check weather for the week.

- Car inspected, oil is changed, and tires have the correct pressure.

- Check airline luggage restrictions.

- Download Apps needed for your trip.

Right Before Leaving

- Contact bank and credit cards to tell them your location.

- Clean out refrigerator.

- Empty garbage cans.

- Lock windows.

- Make sure you have the proper identification with you.

- Bring cash for tips.

- Remember travel documents.

- Lock door behind you.

- Remember wallet.

- Unplug items in house and pack chargers.

- Change your thermostat settings.

- Charge electronics, and prepare camera memory cards.

READ OTHER GREATER THAN A TOURIST BOOKS

Greater Than a Tourist- Geneva Switzerland: 50 Travel Tips from a Local by Amalia Kartika

Greater Than a Tourist- St. Croix US Birgin Islands USA: 50 Travel Tips from a Local by Tracy Birdsall

Greater Than a Tourist- San Juan Puerto Rico: 50 Travel Tips from a Local by Melissa Tait

Greater Than a Tourist – Lake George Area New York USA: 50 Travel Tips from a Local by Janine Hirschklau

Greater Than a Tourist – Monterey California United States: 50 Travel Tips from a Local by Katie Begley

Greater Than a Tourist – Chanai Crete Greece: 50 Travel Tips from a Local by Dimitra Papagrigoraki

Greater Than a Tourist – The Garden Route Western Cape Province South Africa: 50 Travel Tips from a Local by Li-Anne McGregor van Aardt

Greater Than a Tourist – Sevilla Andalusia Spain: 50 Travel Tips from a Local by Gabi Gazon

Children's Book: *Charlie the Cavalier Travels the World* by Lisa Rusczyk Ed. D.

57

> TOURIST

Follow us on Instagram for beautiful travel images:
http://Instagram.com/GreaterThanATourist

Follow *Greater Than a Tourist* on Amazon.

>Tourist Podcast

>T Website

>T Youtube

>T Facebook

>T Goodreads

>T Amazon

>T Mailing List

>T Pinterest

>T Instagram

>T Twitter

>T SoundCloud

>T LinkedIn

>T Map

> TOURIST

At *Greater Than a Tourist*, we love to share travel tips with you. How did we do? What guidance do you have for how we can give you better advice for your next trip? Please send your feedback to GreaterThanaTourist@gmail.com as we continue to improve the series. We appreciate your constructive feedback. Thank you.

METRIC CONVERSIONS

TEMPERATURE

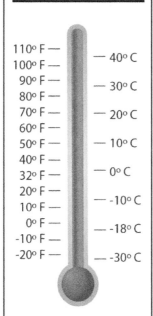

110° F — — 40° C
100° F —
90° F — — 30° C
80° F —
70° F — — 20° C
60° F —
50° F — — 10° C
40° F —
32° F — — 0° C
20° F —
10° F — — -10° C
0° F —
-10° F — — -18° C
-20° F — — -30° C

To convert F to C:

Subtract 32, and then multiply by 5/9 or .5555.

To Convert C to F:

Multiply by 1.8 and then add 32.

32F = 0C

LIQUID VOLUME

To Convert:...............Multiply by
U.S. Gallons to Liters................ 3.8
U.S. Liters to Gallons 26
Imperial Gallons to U.S. Gallons 1.2
Imperial Gallons to Liters....... 4.55
Liters to Imperial Gallons 22
1 Liter = .26 U.S. Gallon
1 U.S. Gallon = 3.8 Liters

DISTANCE

To convert ....Multiply by
Inches to Centimeters 2.54
Centimeters to Inches 39
Feet to Meters....................... .3
Meters to Feet 3.28
Yards to Meters 91
Meters to Yards 1.09
Miles to Kilometers 1.61
Kilometers to Miles............ .62
1 Mile = 1.6 km
1 km = .62 Miles

WEIGHT

1 Ounce = .28 Grams
1 Pound = .4555 Kilograms
1 Gram = .04 Ounce
1 Kilogram = 2.2 Pounds

63

TRAVEL QUESTIONS

- Do you bring presents home to family or friends after a vacation?

- Do you get motion sick?

- Do you have a favorite billboard?

- Do you know what to do if there is a flat tire?

- Do you like a sun roof open?

- Do you like to eat in the car?

- Do you like to wear sun glasses in the car?

- Do you like toppings on your ice cream?

- Do you use public bathrooms?

- Did you bring a cell phone and does it have power?

- Do you have a form of identification with you?

- Have you ever been pulled over by a cop?

- Have you ever given money to a stranger on a road trip?

- Have you ever taken a road trip with animals?

- Have you ever gone on a vacation alone?

- Have you ever run out of gas?

- If you could move to any place in the world, where would it be?

- If you could travel anywhere in the world, where would you travel?

- If you could travel in any vehicle, which one would it be?

- If you had three things to wish for from a magic genie, what would they be?

- If you have a driver's license, how many times did it take you to pass the test?

- What are you the most afraid of on vacation?

- What do you want to get away from the most when you are on vacation?

- What foods smell bad to you?

- What item do you bring on ever trip with you away from home?

- What makes you sleepy?

- What song would you love to hear on the radio when you're cruising on the highway?

- What travel job would you want the least?

- What will you miss most while you are away from home?

- What is something you always wanted to try?

- What is the best road side attraction that you ever saw?

- What is the farthest distance you ever biked?

- What is the farthest distance you ever walked?

- What is the weirdest thing you needed to buy while on vacation?

- What is your favorite candy?

- What is your favorite color car?

- What is your favorite family vacation?

- What is your favorite food?

- What is your favorite gas station drink or food?

- What is your favorite license plate design?

- What is your favorite restaurant?

- What is your favorite smell?

- What is your favorite song?

- What is your favorite sound that nature makes?

- What is your favorite thing to bring home from a vacation?

- What is your favorite vacation with friends?

- What is your favorite way to relax?

- Where is the farthest place you ever traveled in a car?

- Where is the farthest place you ever went North, South, East and West?

- Where is your favorite place in the world?

- Who is your favorite singer?

- Who taught you how to drive?

- Who will you miss the most while you are away?

- Who if the first person you will contact when you get to your destination?

- Who brought you on your first vacation?

- Who likes to travel the most in your life?

- Would you rather be hot or cold?

- Would you rather drive above, below, or at the speed limited?

- Would you rather drive on a highway or a back road?

- Would you rather go on a train or a boat?

- Would you rather go to the beach or the woods?

TRAVEL BUCKET LIST

1.

2.

3.

4.

5.

6.

7.

8.

9.

10.

NOTES

Printed in Great Britain
by Amazon